Look at All the Colors Hidden There

Copyright © Suzanne Burns 2025
All rights reserved.

ISBN 978-0-913123-38-6

Library of Congress Control Number: 2025948122

FIRST PUBLISHED BY GALILEO PRESS IN 2025

Aiken, South Carolina
online at www.freegalileo.com

Interior design by Adam Robinson
Cover art by Suzanne Burns
Cover design by William Akin

Look at All the Colors Hidden There

Suzanne Burns

GALILEO PRESS
Aiken, South Carolina

CONTENTS

Part One

Frequency	11
Trouble	12
The Lion on the Left—	13
I Am What I Amethyst	15
Blood She Must Have	16
Blow Pop	17
Black Bows	18
Celestial Mechanics	19
Dahlias	21
The Aerialist	22
Time Zones	23
The Purgatory Between Memory and Possibility	25
The Cake	26
Bones	28
Such Beautiful Shirts	29
New Year	30
Double Date	31
James Dean	32
Your Watch	35

The Conjuror	36
Electricity	37
Amor Fati	38
Anthesis	39
Happy Hour	43
The Breaking of New Blooms	45
Dahlias, Part 2	47
Dinnertime	48
Eternally Turquoise	49
The Spell	51
Phenology	53
Tourbillon	54

Part Two

Entangled	59
Conversance	60
First Contact	61
Thursday Afternoon	62
Autograph	63
Woman Ahead of Me in the Checkout Line on a Mid-December Night	64
Ashes	65
Memento	67

Passionfruit	68
The Day After	69
Making Up	70
Night Feeding	71
The Offering	72
New Parents	73
About the Freckle	74
First Supper	75
Rose Pajamas	76
Our First Friday Night Alone	77
Last Meeting	78
Meditation in a Chinese Garden	79
A Summer Place	80
Smalltown	82
Courthouse	83
Yes	85
The Night Before the Elopement	86
'til Death Do Us	87
I Do	88
Acknowledgements	*91*
About the Author	*93*

Part One

Frequency

I modulate a signal through the dead air
tuned to a frequency
only you can hear

knowing
other lonely women in love
transmit their own energy,
their own magnetism,
across the high desert,

our signals
the ghost notes of the song
that gallops ahead
of the beat.

The tune I can never get out of my head.

The maximum impulse.
The next big hit.

Trouble

My trouble wants to meet your trouble.
Under my flowered dress I hide mine
the way Bukowski hid his bluebird
though at night instead of singing,
my trouble orders neon pink panties online
while standing in front of the freezer
eating chocolate ice cream off my thumb.

You would like the way my trouble
vacillates between contemplating
the movie where Ben Quick
dreams of waltzing Clara around
a church social under the moon—
my trouble is the egg blue ribbon he insists
she tie in her hair—to wondering
if she could ever sympathize with Ilse Koch.

My trouble thinks Buchenwald
sounds like the name of the Huntsman
who couldn't bear to cut out
Snow White's heart
in the center of the Black Forest
where my trouble daydreams
of finding your trouble
whittling a branch into a point
just sharp enough.

The Lion on the Left—

who lives inside a Paris museum
stores my wish for you
deep inside an ear with a top tuft
tailor-made for secrets
a year before your kiss
changed the contours of my face.

I stroll through the Salon of Dogs
towards the Cabinet of the Wolf
with a husband unable to enjoy
the stuffed polar bear
because a hungry man
is sleeping near the front gate.

I am secretly starving for you
through the museum film
about monkeys and bananas.

Can we buy some for the man?
How do we order bananas in French?

My husband, so troubled
about bananas, unable to seek
the syrupy comfort of *crème brulee*,
the wonders of Parisian
grocery store puddings,
while others go without,

you unaware that if I tell you
what I whispered in the lion's ear—
not one thing about bananas—
you will understand
all the nights I spent refusing
to dream of you
as you began each day
on the other side of my hip.

I Am What I Amethyst

The first love letter I send you,
my nails ten sapphires polished
the shade of the Hope Diamond
when it still sat as the third eye
in a statue of Sita,

just because you asked,

or if this legend,
like most, is untrue,
ten blue valentines ready
to blow you ten blue kisses
the catastrophic shade
of the jewel
as it slumbered in an Indian mine,

unnamed and of the earth
before the curses, the museums,
the replica in that movie
about the ship and the iceberg.

Blood She Must Have

I ask you not to make it bloody
but you make it as bloody
as this beating thing between us,
a medium-rare steak set before me
when I come to your restaurant
with a coterie of vegans.

Your currency is meat, manager
at the best steakhouse in town.
What is it about a woman
who likes eating salad that makes
men so uncomfortable?

Others have tried tempting me
with *tacos al carbon* in Mexico,
steak au poivre in France,
a ribeye bleeding into the eggs
on a diner plate of another man
impressed by his own fatness.

I've never even seen you eat
but I like the way you test
my allegiance to this new game
while no one in my old religion
of broccoli and kale
laughs at the first joke
only you and I are in on.

Blow Pop

Gamboling on the edge
of my stained lips, more cherry
than a cherry blossom
but much less red than a first kiss,
I photograph my mouth on the verge
of a hard bite down,

the tip of my tongue taking
Nabokov's trip,
the sticky white wrapper
I press like a flower in a book
I may not find again

until we both forget to remember
the afternoon I sent a photo
of my mouth to your phone,

the pink and purple flash,

both of us old enough to understand
in the hand of a woman
a lollipop
is always a dangerous act.

Black Bows

Black-bowed shoes shipped
from Guangzhou just to please you.

Doodled bows
across all my journal pages.
Loopy black hearts
with black arrows pierced through.
This hidden archery of ink
catapulting us towards delight,
these smeared bows tying together
all the want I aim towards you.

One black bow on a white shirt
I sew in place the night before
mostly just to see
whether I can still be a distraction.

The first bowed photo I send, eager
to be made more real
by the documentation
of your eyes on my left thigh,
so late one night, us
both alone,
tiny black tie on the side
of that one pair of panties.

Celestial Mechanics

I paint my nails the color of Tang
to bring out the astronaut in you.
How very John Glenn
to take my hand and waltz me away
from the nearest black hole.
You will speak of stars
collapsing in on themselves
and I will joke about vacuums,
how nature abhors them
and how Steinbeck
called them sweeping machines
unplugged but grazing
across a rug in *Tortilla Flat*.

You do not need to be an astronaut
for me to clean up after you.

My mother poured Tang each morning,
feeding me the promise
of a cosmic future fueled by vitamin C,
in the 70s heaven easier to reach
with all of us so pretty,
with Archie so disgruntled
in his whiteness on TV,
with you so unknown
it would take an astronaut
a mini-series to drive his Corvette
between our homes.

What did your father do while my father
in his uniform each morning traded
one theatre for another
as my body pulled the nutrition
from glass after glass of the sour stuff
years before our teenage selves
rocketed down back roads
in cars with backseats
soft as a mother's lap?

What I would give
to have been a kid with you.
One Friday night. One football game
I pretended to watch, touchdowns
memorized from the radio
so I could sneak away
with my Designer Imposters body spray
and my Supertramp.

Remember on the cover, the waitress
who could be anybody's mother
with her real orange juice
fresh squeezed,
the missed elixir I am trying
to get back to as my fingernails
become ten polished orange beacons
guiding you past a new Kármán Line
to the edge of a very unexpected place.

Dahlias

Golden honeycombs, you text, then tell me
you want to move to Chicago
where we can live in an apartment
with a medicine cabinet in the bathroom

and wouldn't I look gorgeous
putting on mascara in front of the mirror
as your wife comes home from work
in day-old office makeup
wondering who will offer to cook dinner.

Dresden, primrose, sulfur, maize.

Are there yellow flowers,
or flowers of any color,
on some table in the pink house
where I hope you sleep alone

every night like you say?

The Aerialist

You tell me the sky tonight
is a wanting by Titian—
Bacchus, Ariadne, and her crown of stars—
as I wait to perform more tricks for you.

Then you correct yourself.
Not a wanting, but a painting.

The moon divides our Elizabethan houses
as we hoist my trapeze past
old telephone bills and wedding vows.

Without a net you show me the brutality
of a sky that speaks of separation.

There is no mercy.

Time Zones

1.
Early autumn in farm country
the moon finds its scene over the fields
an hour before it finds you,
separated by miles and marriages
and now Mountain Time.

We have this thing about the moon,
more like sailors on the same ship
than lovers divided by time zones,
each of us rigging the head, the jib,
on a stage the ocean swell
shaped from wood,
painted blue, one of us
on either side mimicking the tide.

2.
Do you see it, the bandage
pulled off, the blood moon,
the moon whose lunar seas
turn red while you sleep?

Sea of Crises, Sea of Tranquility,
Ocean of Storms,
Sea that has Become Unknown,
Sea of Nectar,

and we forgive each other
for never being in the same place.

3.
I stand on the porch in shadow
wishing for your long fingers
to know my body so well
the novelty of my small waist
will give away, in the darkness,
to a new syntax created
from the way your hands
read the Braille of my bones.

4.
Some nights I even study
the ring around the moon.
The old myth of bad weather coming,
a sailor's warning.
The new myth of Sisyphus,
both of us pushing the moon up the sky
only to have it fall back on our faces.

The Purgatory Between Memory and Possibility

Your memory clings
like one of those scorned ghosts
in a Japanese horror film.

Shredded rice paper curtains,
retribution,
generations of a specific,
broken-hearted menace.

You balance on, before becoming,
the slide between being always with me
and never with me,
my black phone tucked
beneath my pillow
so I can dream you are more
than a few scattered sentences
texted when no one is looking.

The Cake

Your wife arrived at my reading
carrying a white cake
crowned in white sugar roses
like someone in the audience
was having a surprise wedding.

A gift to me for encouraging your writing.
A peace offering to you, her bid
to be kind to the one who supported
your poems, late at night,
while she slept and we emailed
edits back and forth. Only edits.

She told you she baked the cake.
Watched a tutorial, paid for a lesson,
described how to test
for the doneness of crumb.
What an achievement,
her icy sheen of buttercream.
She ordered pans, she said, a cake tester,
scraped the seeds from a real vanilla bean.

I saw the same cake for sale in the window
of the only bakery downtown
and I wondered about you
and I wondered about her
and I knew she and I could never
be friends as the years passed
and I lost track of what you and she

took turns lying to each other about,
keeping her secret to myself
until now.

Bones

Beneath my lace shirt my clavicle
waits to be noticed,
its collar around my neck straining
towards your spectacular blue shirt.

In that one embrace my thoracic curve
box steps towards yours better
than Fred and Ginger in *Swing Time*.

Of course my heart tattoos
beneath my bones
when your blue shirt nears
but what about the twelve hearts
sitting inside my spine,
our vertebrae faceted together
in bony gossip as they conspire
to break each other open,
touch the hard love tokens inside.

Your skeleton
eases towards me before your heart
has a chance to catch up.
I arrange my body in the fashion of flesh
waiting for your bones to undress.

My locked jaw, my clicking ribs,
how they realign to accept yours,
the brutal crush of symmetry,
the ease of a perfect fit.

Such Beautiful Shirts

I understand the direction
of the pattern of any shirt
you wear with a pattern

and even the direction
of every thread
on every button

and how, if I could be alone with your shirts,

I would mark
one hidden button on each
with a silver thread
so the world, and your shirts,
would know I passed by.

New Year

Party favors burst their joy across midnight.

The woman who rules you on paper
will kiss you for show,
for sport, for drunkenness
as I wait for you to call
upon my lips the way
a chorus waits to find its bridge.

The way the bridge I crossed
the afternoon my mouth took its turn
waits for us to come back.

The way with that one kiss
we forgot about the rulers, their papers,
as you asked if I knew
the names of the birds
waiting to whisper our date in my ear.

Double Date

We went on a double date once.
She pretended to like me
and he bought you a beer
after you left your wallet at home.

We sat through a play.
She refused to laugh
and I could hear only your laugh.

On the way home my husband
told me he did not like your wife.
You should not be stuck in a house
with a woman who never laughed.

I told him she looked expensive.
She smelled of flowery perfume.
She did not need to laugh.

No, he said.
There is someone else out there waiting for him.

Someone he will never see coming.

James Dean

There is not much left to say
except if he sat on a swing
we would all wait in line to push him.

You are from Indiana, so you know these things.

A father would question
what about him made
a daughter lose her mind.

A mother would primp
in the backseat of a Buick.

Your Uncle Richard would apologize
for stealing Jimmy's tombstone
twenty years after his death
to charge neighbor kids
a quarter per viewing.

Directors would pitch scripts.

Tabloids would reveal the photo
in his wallet.
(Sal Mineo or Pier Angeli?)

Elizabeth Taylor would drop
her handful of teeth dug
from Monty Clift's throat
to barter for a chance to take cuts.

Robert Frost would write a poem
about almost not waiting in line,
how he could choose the empty swing.
(This would make no difference.)

Peggy would carry
an autograph dog for him to sign.

Mark David Chapman would search
for some new beauty to destroy.

A baker would make his dozen
because he was up anyway.

Kay and Porky would return
the stolen graveside bottles,
the joints, the cigarettes,
the pocketed lipsticks,
Revlon's Cherries in the Snow,
tucked among the faded flowers.

My cousin would cut to the front
because blondes are greedy for fun.

Mechanics would take bets
on the whereabouts,
cursed or not cursed,
of Little Bastard.

Look, there's my husband.
There's your wife.
The lover, the uncle,
the hostess,
the girl who sends you panties in the mail,
the man who works at Safeway
and wants to kiss me in the cantaloupe

as you lead me away from the crowd
to a shaded spot beneath a sycamore tree.

Your Watch

Bruise of your left wrist,
wound
I refuse to notice or tend,
that black mar
on your field of pale skin,

your watch
could be such a better watch
if she wasn't always waiting
at the other end.

The Conjuror

You write a poem about your wife.
You never show me the poem
and I never ask to see.

It was something, you say, about her
and ribbons pinned to a heart,
a voodoo doll you two
take turns sticking to see
who draws first blood.

How thoughtless, to talk about her
being your muse.
She is too ordinary to star in any poem
but this is what writers do,

vampire the essence
out of anyone within reach.

You do it to me, I do it to you.

Electricity

Your hand on my knee
is the true invention of electricity,

the knee who has walked me
around cities where I struggled
to understand the coin
jingling in my palm,
how to hail a cab,

my left leg almost keeping up,
lagging a little behind

until you started something burning
between my femur and tibia,
your fingered swords hitting
the sweet spot in my stone
that always reminds me of catching
subways in foreign cities,

the rush of movement
when your train approaches your track
and you know, for that one hour
on that one afternoon,
you were never lost.

Amor Fati

If you were only bones

and your bones, someday,
took up residence
in a science class
I would break in at night
to twirl you around the room

until Love asked me to,
please,
love you a little less.

Anthesis

O, patterns.
O, predictable omen.
O, harbinger.
O, grip in the night downward
pressed on the right lung, unclasped
as I wake with a start.

You blossom me
in a tight white dress.
There are certain fabrics that come
into a woman's life only once or twice
and alter the history of her dimensions.

There are certain men who come,
and if I could predict such anthesis
waited for me would I have crept
into that unfinished house
overlooking our town butte
long-ago on a teenage night?

O, coercion.
O, odes to compulsion.
O, the earring curved in a silver snake
I lost in the car of a boy
who promised me
just the right amount of nothing,
my young heart troubled
inside its bony xylophone,
more tender than the love token
the Woodsman couldn't bear bring his queen.

As I unfold my body before a camera lens,
little black shoes, little white dress,
I think of cherry trees
and if you would like the first girl I kissed,
such a pale terror, all cheekbones, black hair,

Chekhov's Anya in our college play,
her lips in a Russian lisp
we rehearsed at night before we slept
with no idea how
to really open each other.

And where were you the night
the girl and I abandoned
the orchard as we turned
our sweet secrets from each other
decades before you explained
why a cherry tree is never a cherry tree
and always a cherry tree
and only a cherry tree,

mono no aware as I raise my curves in the air
and wonder if a photo of longing will translate.

O, fleeting chance for delight.
O, death, but not quite yet.
O, fleshy drupe, the red center pit
of my exposed heart.

O, petals to conceal the overripe fruit
among all my grateful, quivering filaments.

You should see how my anthers can dance.

O, how you notice pink blossoms
outside the window.
O, the maddening rushes of *almost*.
O, when you say close
do we still mean *thisclose*?

Even the ghosts that time
the descent of living stop their watches
when you speak of petals,
like Pound's,
like Neruda's,
turning themselves over
in the heartbroken mischief
of Romance languages.

O, when you gesture towards flowers
how I see the blue beyond the pink.
O, *nel blu dipinto di blu*.
O, how your volar waves in understated grace.
O, Dean Martin crooning "Volare"
on the stead of Sinatra urging us to see
what Spring is like on Jupiter and Mars.

O, open the calyx and see all the sepals.
O, pistil. O, stamen.
O, to lounge on a bed
with my thighs ready to rule you.

O, patterns.

It makes a woman forget all this talk
of unfulfilled longing
in favor of befriending
the nearest bird.

There are feathers,
miraculous in their patterns.

A whole world still hidden
beneath my surface.

Happy Hour

My best friend doesn't like coming
to happy hour anymore,
even with all the free food.

She will drink and eat anything
you offer, bits of steak, chocolate torte,
an occasional top-shelf bourbon,
extra lemonade, extra dressing,
extra baby tomatoes
on the Caesar salad that never
comes with tomatoes.

Why leave a plumber
for a restaurant manager?
How many charcuterie boards
equal new pipes in an old duplex?

She once asked if you knew
how to fix a sink, why your wife sits
at the other end of the dining room
when she comes to eat for free, too?

Why she never stops by our table to say hello?

She does not measure men
by their ability to write poems,
asking through mouthfuls
of whatever substitution you've delivered,
what if someday I want

to learn how to play the accordion?

I tell her I can buy my own accordion.

The Breaking of New Blooms

I stand in a daze just outside
the fence when my husband takes over
my job of watering the garden.
A garden you don't even know about,
once enflamed in plumes of cockscomb,
pepperbox poppies, the whispering
pinks of candytuft and milkweed
ringed in butterhead and romaine.

We start making salads again
with store-bought lettuce.
Lost in thoughts of you
I forgot to plant the seeds,
cradled in a kind of nostalgia
for the way you once told me
about a summer moon tinged silver,
your lifelong desire to create
a blooming night garden
of lamb's ear and iceberg roses,
jasmine opening as the sun sets.

I will wait to hear you speak
to me again about the moon
while all the gardens of the world
fold in on themselves,
long after everyone forgets
about every growing season,
long after everyone forgets
the song about standing alone

under a blue moon,
the song about the rose and its thorn,
the song about crossing
the moon river in style,
and even the book about tucking
the tired moon to sleep.

Dahlias, Part 2

Now when I see flower huts
along the roadside I think of you
and the dahlias you planted
when you tried to reconcile
with your wife before realizing
she will never notice

and sometimes I even think
of Sylvia waiting
to bite Ted on the cheek,
their first meeting.
Waiting for him to demand
her hair band,
her pearl earring,
his insistence they play for keeps

and how knowing him
turned her poems into currency,
coaxed her to find verse
in the moon and a yew tree
the way you make me better

as much as a temporary
kind of love can be earned,
as much as ruminations
on churning the butter
of daffodils in their backyard,
such a rare earth smell,
can conceal the hatred
between every man and every woman.

Dinnertime

I wonder if your wife
knows where I live
and if she is coming for me
like she promised
until I remember
watching her in the deli line
trying to decide between
potato salad or ambrosia,
her large purse stuffed
with receipts and candy bars
falling to the floor,
her Wonder Woman water bottle
no one bothered to help her pick up.

Eternally Turquoise

For a few hours you let me believe
you were mine, the moon
when I left you the kind of moon
no one notices,
milky blemish on the night sky
as I came to you with a pale blue moon
at the end of each fingertip.

You are careless with me
the way only a married man
can be to the married woman
who secretly loves him,
who spends too much on makeup
and happy hour clothes to come
see you while your wife
never dresses up for bed,
tossing her monthly blood stains
in the laundry
with your best shirt.

I buy another blue polish
though I prefer red.

In the photo from your Christmas party
your wife's cherry polish
is chipped to small red dots
in the center of each nail,
as if with an editing pen
you marked her

the same way you wrap
around her in the picture,
your long arms circling
this woman you swear
is trying to kill you.

Why?

The Spell

I clip my hair and slit a finger,
wrap the bloody braid
around a chocolate lily.

I want to grow something,
a spell to keep you close.

My sister once buried
a found ring in a beer can
near where I stoop,
attempting to claim
the Druid part of me
with my little wreath of dark hair
tucked in the earth.

A spell to change the legacy
of men who think they have loved me,
another childless mother
who collects jewelry
instead of babies.

The pearls I've never worn.
A brooch someone gave me
at a cafe when I was young.
The rings before the first wedding ring.
The pendant from someone after.

No gem holds its luster
like the intertwined fortress of hair,
the blood it wears like a mantle,
something so old-fashioned
about a woman casting her net
into the chilled night air,
waiting to see
what hope brings back.

Phenology

When you think of me,
just once in the snow,
my body will be summer blush,
the petal of a wishing rose,
the smell of sugared jelly.

Lean close,
my hair no longer hair
but the rope in stories
men long to climb.

I am waiting at the top of a tower
built more from grieving than from stone.

Look at all the colors hidden there.

See the slow movement
of cream spilled along the floor.

Taste that one drop of honey.

Tourbillon

1.
There is a light at the end of this poem
that calls to all the other poems
while Robert Frost gets lost in this book,
wondering what would happen
if James Dean sped down a different road…

I give this light to you, rescued
from the bottom of the trash
when I cut my hair this morning,
remembering the bench in the park,
the water the afternoon I touched
my head to your shoulder
and there were no lights
because I was too full of living
to care about poems.

2.
Lafcadio's Yuki-onna in the summer.
You promised not to tell, and you told.

3.
Last night I brought the rain,
this morning woke to coyotes
howling in the meadow,
close, and found
a rabbit's foot on my porch,
a rabbit's tail sitting beside,
the sweetbreads discarded in a grey havoc

I cleaned with an old rag
and a bowl of warm water,
a penance for calling
the wildness of you to the wildness of me.

4.

I knew she would come back.
The me before you.
She was waiting in the dark
when I shopped for dresses
and lipsticks and fingernail paint.

5.

Regret can snuff out
the wick at the end of the poem,
but I only feel sad
about having to step aside,
make room for her to push me
out of the way when I'm zipping up my skirt.
What a catastrophe.

6.

Mira que si te quise, fué por el pelo.
Ahora que estás pelona, ya no te quiero.

7.

My hair in the trash, great handfuls
golden at the tips.
The hair of remembrance
I'm too sad to remember.

Elegiac hair.
Scarred hair.
Proustian hair.

I blow warmly on my handfuls
until there is smoke.

Part Two

Entangled

After you leave your wife
I try on every skirt I own
as if a cut or ruffle or polka dot
will know the charm
to keep me safe.
When you tell me not to come to you,

not yet,

I stand alone in a grocery line,
thigh pressed
into the cold grid of my cart
as I self-check ice cream
I will take one bite of and throw away
before settling under my blanket
near my candy bars and Kleenex,

my skirts folded
and placed back in the closet
as if no one out of the ordinary
were expecting them.

Conversance

The tips of my fingertips to yours,

finally,

say more than all the letters
lovers have written,

even the one hidden
in that jewelry box
somewhere in Nebraska
with the little ballerina
who pirouettes
when her girl opens the lid,

checking that morning,
for the eighteenth time,
to make sure the note from him
is still tucked inside.

First Contact

When you move inside me
I can't help but think of men
who fall in love with statues,
water nymphs, mermaids,
the little bronze boy for eternity bent
and set to release his little bronze boat
into the pond that embraces him,

the historical figures
everyone else has forgotten,
the voluptuousness hidden in bodies
that are almost real,
something the men in love with statutes
can never quite explain,

and if I knew you a little better
I would weep when your body
falls from mine, me, a woman
still crying for the men
in love with statues because, together
in a dim room on a dark side road,
you and I are almost too close
to leave space for anyone else
to reach for the nearest person
and hope they reach back.

Thursday Afternoon

We abandon
six pitted apricots
on a maple cutting board
we will never get back to
as you press my hip
against the kitchen counter
to the sound of a running faucet
we forget to turn off.

Autograph

The tongue that makes me
understand the vulgar
Latin of romance languages,
your breath an exhale of grief
as my other life forces me
to leave the comfort of you,
my body wears the unexpected
pink pleasures of your teeth,
autographs after the eternity
of boys who signed the wrong things
at the ends of letters and school years
and on those goofy grinning dogs
the girls who loved Elvis
once took to bed to inch
under the covers,
not really understanding
the need to feel something
almost alive between the furls.

Woman Ahead of Me in the Checkout Line on a Mid-December Night

I stood behind your cart
of hairspray and cat food
as you turned to snicker
at the contraband clutched
in my hands—pink panties
stamped in little glitter skulls.

I am still trying to find love
even alone at night after a day of him.

This search might kill me,
but it's still better than being a woman
who buys Christmas napkins
months before the holidays

to cross another chore off your list,
to make sure your pantry stays full.

Ashes

1.

Your wife sends your mother's ashes
to your work the night your smalltown hero
sings across the river, Mellencamp
on a stop to our Oregon woods
while you finish your shift with a large box
waiting to walk you home.

Your wife's last pierce to the heart
of a good night reminiscing
about your mother's favorite,
who grew up in the same town as you.
She knew the location of the little pink house
running on continuous MTV repeat,
her Indiana doo-wop, her Midwest Elvis,
your wife knowing
when you asked for your things back
you did not mean this.

2.

The day I meet your mother she is sitting
on your writing desk in a box
with a hinged lid, almost like a large pencil case
tucked between your books and pens.

You never call to ask your wife
why she took the ashes.
An iris blooms in the side yard—
the first flower in twenty years.

3.
You mother haunts your dreams
so I bring her home, open the lid, once,
to see the rumor of tiny, unburned bones.
I place the ashes between
my own books and pens.
My husband knows not to ask

4.
While everyone sleeps in my house and
    yours
I research what to do with ashes,
decide on a burial at sea,
pay the three hundred dollars
from my husband's savings.

5.
The girl who works at the post office
cries as she places the orange
Cremated Remains
sticker on the side of the box.

I ship your mother to the Washington coast.
A sea burial. They send back a document
with a seal and coordinates.

Full fathom five, I think, and bring
you the paper the next time
I sneak away to see you
in exchange for the promise
to block your wife's number.

Memento

The afternoon you snore in bed
an hour before I have to go back
to my other life I am filled
with such tenderness
for all the moments we could show
each other no tenderness
yet still make it to the afternoon
of me watching you sleep
that I take a picture of you,
the man I have never seen sleep.
I curse your dreams
for taking you away from me,
the covers pulled back just enough
so I pull them back a little more,
wait for light to illuminate
your face,
your left nipple,
your forearm bent either in peace
or in a beginning flex
to push the weight of possibility off you
the moment I dare turn your body,
your face,
into a keepsake
to love the way women
once loved men in photographs
sent off to war
who promise to return.

Passionfruit

Ravenous, I finger the fruit
on your nightstand that smells
of Oahu, where I grew up,
our silhouette of sweat drying
to salt on the red sheets
you wrap over me on the occasions
we get under something
instead of over each other
a week before one blonde hair
from your new secret lover
coiled between us means
there will be no more satin,
our small bed stretched
into an ocean I am still trying
to swim my way back to.

The Day After

I will not let the new woman
I find you with ruin
how I love you the way
little kids love packs of valentines,
and angels, I believe, love
always being right.

I still love the shirt I bought
that made her notice you
and the brain that tricked you
into thinking this is something
I can get over,
but maybe it's the blue polish
that keeps me going?

The new watch I gave you.
The way you looked at me
that one time when the sun
stuck in the sky like a drawing
a mother who loves the artist
tapes on the wall for a very long time.

Making Up

The slow, simple lick
of a shared ice cream cone
that keeps us going
the still afternoon
Gothic writers venerate,

lilacs in bloom
on the next block
as you steal a flower
from the neighbor's yard

in your mind meant for me,
a small sun sinking
into the weeds you rescue
with your touch.

Something about the way
you offer me the thieved blossom,
held beyond the prickled stem,
almost alarming where I touch,
becomes a promise that the next flower
will not say *I'm sorry*
or *forgive me*
or anything at all.

Night Feeding

I eat potato chips over the sink
as the snow,
and my marriage,
keep us apart,

knowing the exact day
my love for you turned me
into a woman
who eats and cries,

careful over the sink late at night
while everyone is sleeping
not to inhale cookie crumbs
or choke on an errant olive pit

though I prefer the sound of potato chips
filling the house with the precise,
brutal crunch of a woman
who longs for her lover

so I keep chewing
in a secret pact with myself
as I draw a napkin across my face,
careful not to wipe away
all the places you've been.

The Offering

On the bed after hours of pulling
our bodies to fit each other,
practicing how to say,
this time, please,
don't leave,
my shoes too heavy,
my sweater melted on your floor,
a big, soft pearl shucked
off my body when our afternoon
held the promise of time,
I bite into a pear, testing
its sweetness before I hand you
the wet, bruised fruit,
part offering, part apology
as we tear into
the sugared flesh, almost ripe,
almost in season,
back and forth
in a striptease to reach the dark seeds
before my mouth, fruit heavy,
presses against your mouth,
not the same way it found your lips
during the day's beginning
when neither of us checked
our watches, my mouth searching
for your mouth now to make sure
both of us keep breathing,
that forced smile as I stand to leave,
that last grit of skin between our teeth.

New Parents

We name the jackfruit
you bring into the house
on the kind of day too hot
to do anything but stare
at the giant green creature
resting on the counter between us.

Bumpy, sharp-stemmed,
cumbersome,
we talk to him the way
we would soothe a baby
too fussy to care about
my favorite lullaby,
some boy named Michael
with a nickel to spend
on more sweets
than he could ever imagine,
as if the promise of candy
is something he will take
his whole life to accept,

until the heat takes hold
and death blooms before us
so you find a safe spot
in the yard behind a rock
for our fleeting progeny
to go back to the soil he came from
while you tell me not to look.

About the Freckle

Dark little imp,
tiny mark of promise
alerting both of us
we are each made up of so much skin,
your gentle finger signing
a peace treaty.

O, exalted blemish,
please watch over us this time around.

Please protect us

if we fail to remember
the afternoon you became
more than just a freckle
but the first word in a prayer
for nothing more
but the possibility of more.

First Supper

The afternoon I leave my husband
we sit in a diner
holding hands while others
chew without talking, unaware
the flush on their right shoulder,
warm pulse down left leg
like the burn
of an overworked muscle
is us.

The fuse, the match,
the Big Bang of leg against leg
as we fumble
through the pie menu
before giving up,
all of life becoming a dessert
we cannot believe we deserve.

Rose Pajamas

I buy rose pajamas
after fleeing my home,
stitched red buds tangled
in the folds as your arms open
like a galaxy
no scientist can comprehend,
bouquet of posies across my right breast
as I arrange my garden
against yours,
red rose-covered thigh
seeking your thigh, the light
on what becomes your side
of the bed a yellow sentry
leading me to sleep.

Our First Friday Night Alone

We rearrange your writing desk
after your wife burns
the signed Robert Coover,
sells the rest of your books, throws
the antique typewriters off the deck.

You replace the ribbon
in the typewriter that survives
the two-story plunge while I straighten
your books and papers,
an old dictionary, a few small volumes
of Japanese poetry smuggled in a jacket.

The vintage desk escaped the wrath.
I don't blame her.
I'd hate us, too.
New love lacks the grace to apologize
to the ones it leaves behind.

Last Meeting

The last time I see my husband he asks
if you do crossword puzzles in pen.
We sit on the inflatable bed
that has become his new life
going over who will pay
future bills, how to divide debt,
love letters, his classic motorcycle,
the large sofa not designed
to break into sections.

He will keep his family and his paychecks.
I will lose a few friends who think
being married to a plumber
is like winning a lottery
of free house calls.

The last time I see my husband
he predicts the new marriage.
Promises I will be a good wife to you.
Thanks me for being kind to his brothers,
for remembering the oldest brother
loved my rum cake,
and for never baking another rum cake
after the brother died.

Meditation in a Chinese Garden

On your forty-fifth birthday
we wander beneath a weeping katsura,
the lacebark, the lily turf.

Love between us means love right now.

Love
as we hold hands too much in the rain
to take photographs of the chrysanthemums.

Love
as water bathes a persimmon fallen off its
    tree.

Love
as my wet coat presses against your wet coat
for the hundredth time.

A Summer Place

Our first summer I stay with you
on weekends, bring my pajamas,
my books, my Sinatra records,
my grocery store flower bouquets,

and we live a small life together
in a thin blue room,

always wet
from the downstairs pool,
always smelling of chlorine
and grilled meat.

People who know me
as part of a different couple
still tell me to say hello to him
when we bicycle through town
for oranges and cheese.

My husband buys a house and chickens.
Your wife calls pretending she is pregnant.

You and I dine on bacon wrapped figs
at the club down the hill, laughing
at a summer rental so close
to swimming pools
and putting greens,

neither of us caring
where the two exes sleep or eat,
or where they are going,
or where they have been.

Smalltown

Over dinner at a Chinese restaurant
we laugh at a friend staring
at us from across the dining room,
how he cups his hand
to the side of his face, blinders
as he walks to the bathroom
while we feed each other chow mein.

When he rises to leave
we ask him to sit with us
as we finish our tea.

We are not having an affair, we say.

I left my husband. He left his wife.
The children know. The pets know.
The bank tellers and grocery clerks know.
In a few more hours
the whole town will know.

Our friend liked me being part
of a different couple.
He liked you having
a wife to complain about.

It's okay, we tell him,
as we break open our fortune cookies.

We don't need them anymore.

Courthouse

A month before Thanksgiving we walk
hand-in-hand into the courthouse.
I do not pause to wonder
who will bake the pecan pies, enough
to feed twenty members
of the family I will leave behind.

Who will sit in the corner and listen
to a nephew's new Jay-Z obsession
while a niece takes selfies.
Who will flip the record
of the brother who brings the records
everyone talks over.

Who will make sure the one
who drinks too much remembers to eat,
and the one who won't eat at least takes
a piece of pie for the road.

Who will find the one knife sharp enough
to cut through the pecans
with a dog begging at their feet.

Who will clear the dishes
during talk of politics, wash away
the cold, thickened blood of the roast plate,
another year's carnage down the drain
as chatter turns to Christmas brunch plans
and New Year's dinner.

I do not stop to wonder about the ones
I left behind. You are not the only one
who has people who want to throw
your things in the street.

Your wife says she will kill herself.
My husband says he understands,
for one moment,
people who want to kill themselves.

But it is too late to go back
to the day before love showed us
to the lawyers who explained
with one piece of paper
we get to start over,

understanding there will be children
who never speak to you again,
a nephew who will soon follow
new bands I've never heard of.
The next person
who signs up to bring the pies
will have to pick them up
from the grocery store.

Yes

You stride towards the front door
with a bouquet of red dahlias
in one hand
and a ring in the other,
orange flame, your birthstone,
surrounded by shine.

You take a knee
under the yellow light
at the edge of my family home,
poise at my threshold
as you wait for me to speak.

The Night Before the Elopement

Halfway between
my old life and a new name,
Reno in the distance
a jewel of fidelity waiting
to be excavated
among the bachelor parties
and pawn shops,
we stay the night in a town
where you show me how to enjoy
rooms with no TV,
Birds and Bees the theme of our suite.

A buzz around your head
seems too poetic not to be planted
by Saint Adelaide,
Patron Saint of Second Marriages,
the end of October in a chilly room
but a bee flits from lamp to bureau
to antique rocking chair,
winter closing in beyond us
on the pale blue sierras,

in here, nothing but spring.

'til Death Do Us

We walk to our chapel past
an abandoned motel with an empty pool,
pawn shops fanning out dozens
of Return to Tiffany pendants,

a royal flush of silver hearts
from all the lonely-hearted women
who can't stop putting coins in machines
and the boyfriends
who once loved them enough
to buy pretty, useless things,

our paces strong, determined
not to be late for our own wedding,
warm afternoon sweat cooling
beneath my tight white shift,

hands heavy with cameras
and wedding rings and adrenaline
calling my nerves to action
when you open the front door
of our downtown strip-mall church
and usher me in.

I Do

I never call you William
but for the ceremony I call you
William
as I slide the thick silver ring
onto your long finger.

A five-minute formality.

On the corner a saxophone busker
balances against a bench.
We dance to the song he plays,
close to the middle of traffic—
I've already forgotten the song
if I ever knew—
and you leave him a tip before
we saunter towards the Truckee River,

its great white, roiling edges
luminescent in sunlight
as if every religion is always,
and is never,
true.

Acknowledgements

One of these love letters, *First Contact*, made its way to Free State Review a few years ago. It was my first poem a literary journal published in ages, and my first contact with Barrett Warner, who is the reason this collection of love letters is now between two covers.

Thank you to my favorite poetry teacher, Gareth Thomson, wherever you are.

Thank you to Matt Love, my first reader when these poems wove into the semblance of a manuscript. So many years ago I told him, when discussing agents and novels and the writing business, how happy it made me to write poems, to which he replied, then go write poems. His two careful edits of the manuscript, not yet fully formed, pushed me to seek publication.

Thank you to Barrett Warner, who pushed the boundaries of what both my poetry and Catholic brain could handle until we broke down the barrier of what a poem could be, why a poem exists in this world, and how to find a place for all these scribblings that started out as desperate thoughts, late at night, when no one else was awake.

A special thank you to Matthew Thomas Meade, who needs no content warning, and who challenged my "final" manuscript edit in ways I never knew my stubborn mind could accept. I threw this book to him in the final hour, a Hail Mary pass, that actually worked. This book is better for it, and for you, so thanks. Dude!

Another special thank you to you, Kevin Clark, for patiently watching as a lot of this drama and mischief unfolded before your eyes. (Sorry!)

Obviously, this book would not exist without my husband (yes, we made it!), the muse of all muses, William Akin. Patient Will, who had the difficult task of reading/offering feedback on poems about himself, in real time, from June 2014, while we were both still married to other people, awkward, until October 2018, when we were married in Reno, Nevada, and celebrated after with strawberry ice cream and pink champagne. A man among men, fixer of every dangling participle and my inability to not fully grasp compound words, inspiration for the best birthday cakes, a true jewel of a person who is also the best server in town without ever having to write down an order.

About the Author

Born in Hawaii, Suzanne Burns currently writes both poetry and fiction in Oregon. Recent books include the short fiction collections *Now It Seems That I Am Not Here at All* (Tailwinds Press) and *The Veneration of Monsters* (Dzanc Books). Her work has been recognized by *Ms. Magazine*, *Publisher's Weekly*, and *Kirkus Reviews*, which named her fiction a Top 100 Book of the Year. In between writing sessions, she bakes competitively and once won third place out of 99 chocolate cakes at the Oregon State Fair Gerry Frank Best Chocolate Cake Competition. Right now she writes about fruit.